ROOM COLON NINE

Madeleine (Yeh Jin) Moon-Chun

ROOM COLON NINE

Author: Madeleine Moon-Chun
Photography: Madeleine Moon-Chun

Eastwind Books | Berkeley | 2025

Published by Eastwind Books of Berkeley
2022 University Avenue, Box 46
Berkeley, CA 94704
www.AsiaBookCenter.com

All text, art and photography by Madeleine Moon-Chun

ISBN: 9781961562103

For Benjamin

The most beautiful part of your body
is where it's headed.

Ocean Vuong, "Someday I'll Love Ocean Vuong"

TABLE OF CONTENTS

GOING, GOING   **59**

Author & Photographer

Madeleine (Yeh-Jin) Moon-Chun is a high school student from Georgia. Her debut poetry collection *Not Made of Lines: Poetic Meditations on Time, Space, & Other Matters* was also published by Eastwind Books of Berkeley in 2024. She is the founding Editor-in-Chief of *Student Pedagogies for Social Change*, a literary magazine spotlighting youth voices on issues surrounding social justice. She is the author of the article "Starting a Teen Journal of Asian American Studies: Teen Voices as Critical Pedagogical Method" in the *Journal of Asian American Studies* (Johns Hopkins University Press), 2024. She is a passionate birder and naturalist. Check out her website, Birding for Beauty, https://www.birdingforbeauty.org/. In her spare time, she likes running, playing board games, and spending time with friends and family.

Acknowledgements

Writing is often perceived as a solitary endeavor. It does, however, take a community to become a writer. I am thankful to the many people who are continuing to teach me how to develop my voice and style.

I would like to thank Tom Painting for being my first writing mentor and wonderful Junior High Humanities teacher. Long after leaving eighth grade, he continues to help me look over my poems and has given me invaluable advice about concision.

Dr. Sarah Schiff, my high school English teacher of two years, has also been such a wonderful writing mentor and role model as someone who balances teaching with creative writing. I am so lucky to be in her creative writing class this year, and I learned so much about what it means to make each word, line break, and form and style choice matter. The word "intentionality" has taken on new meaning in my writing life.

I am very grateful for Dr. Barrington Edwards, teacher for both my US History class and Black History seminar. Every day in class, I am practicing criticality in my writing and thinking—to take nothing at face value and question all that I am presented with. My analytical writing and poetry have benefited immensely from his pedagogical methods.

Ms. Abigail Klima of New American Pathways: I am inspired by her compassion and commitment to her students. And all her after-school program students at International Community School: Their vitality, love of life, and immense kindness and acceptance to one another has given me hope despite the world around us and more reason to keep writing for change.

Thank you to Dr. Kim Mansion, my math teacher, for being so supportive of my poetry. In her class, I also learned that math and poetry aren't so different from each other.

Mandy Moe Pwint Tu was my Ellipsis Writing Workshop instructor for the class entitled Applying Pressure: On Wounds and Literary Ancestry. This workshop widened my scope of contemporary poetry, and I appreciate her teaching.

I would also like to thank Iris Cai, Felix Chen, Jessica Wang—Editors-in-Chief of *Eucalyptus Lit*—and all my fellow poetry and prose editors. I am so inspired by the literary talent of the *Eucalyptus* team, and I am grateful to be part of this good project.

The community at *The Incandescent Review* is unlike any other. I have made wonderful connections and friendships from around the country through being an editor there. A shoutout to Avah Dodson and Fatema Rahaman!

I am so grateful to Dr. Harvey Dong who owns and runs *Eastwind Books of Berkeley*. This is our third book project together.

Lucy Rotenberg, Managing Editor of our school's literary magazine *Blue Rider*, is one of the most enthusiastic, kind, and literary people I have ever met. I am grateful for all the prompts she and Sonia, the Editor-in-Chief, gave—some of the writing I did in that club appears in this collection. I will miss her next year!

Finally, I am endlessly—wordlessly—grateful to my family for their love and support of my writing and life journey. I would like to thank my amazing mother for helping me every step of the way from when I was little, ensuring our house was a haven of literary pursuit and critical education. I am grateful for the wonderfully intellectual conversations we engage in every night at the dinner table. I would like to thank my dad who, despite not being "literature-inclined" (or so he says), reads all my poetry and other writings. And finally, my brother is my life companion, fellow jokester, and the sweetest sibling in the world. He has more kindness than anyone I have known. I hope he likes the title of this collection. I dedicate this book to you. May the force of Room Nine continue to bring us endless laughter and great stories.

Reprints

Several of the poems in this collection were submitted to the 2025 Scholastic Writing Awards and received Regional Silver Key Awards for the Georgia region. They are the following: "Our Beginning," "Where We're Headed," "Chaos Theory," "Cosmic Wishes: A Metamorphosis," "Mantras of Empty Conviction," "Myths of Our Own Meaning," "I Hear They Make Marionettes That Fly Now," "For the Siren, Alone, on the Hill," "What was in Reverse," "Aubade for Our Stars," "Confessions from the Angels of Ephemerality," "Snapshots," and "Origins."

"I Hear They Make Marionettes That Fly Now" was also long-listed for the Dawn Review Prize for Poetry.

The poem, "plight of the captive fish," was previously published in *Fleeting Daze*, issue 3 (2024). "Prologue for the Bird-like Dancer" was previously published in the Paideia School's publication, *Blue Rider*, 2024. "If Ceiling Fans Could Talk" was previously published in *The Incandescent Review*, 2024.

Introduction

Numbers are symbolic parts of our traditions, religions, superstitions, and daily lives. Many buildings in the United States don't include the thirteenth floor in writing, as it is considered unlucky. Three, on the other hand, "is the charm." In Korean tradition, the 100th day after a baby is born is cause for a ceremony and a gathering of the community. In the United States, some of the most important birthdays are when someone turns sixteen, eighteen, twenty–one, and fifty. For many Latin American cultures, girls who turn fifteen have their *quinceañera*. Judaism considers thirteen to be when children reach the age of symbolic adulthood. For many Asian countries, the age sixty is celebrated, as it signifies the person has lived through all twelve zodiac signs five times—once for each different universal element. And the list goes on. While various countries and cultures have their own ceremonious ages and numbers, the overarching current of similarity is the symbolic weight we humans place on numbers.

Being part of the title, the number nine seems to warrant explanation. Nine is the last single digit option. It represents the completion, or culmination, of a cycle as well as the beginning of another. As such, nine invites a sense of closure and reflection. On a more personal note, I was born on the ninth of the month, so I associate nine even more strongly with the concept of beginnings and opportunities for growth and development. Women are typically pregnant for around nine months. The womb, then, is a sort of waiting room or in-between space in which a baby resides before exiting their mother's body, simultaneously entering a world entirely new to them. On the flip side, death on the other end of life is also a room in its own right in that it serves as an exit. Rooms are transitory spaces, providing opportunities for us living beings to come and go and stay awhile in between.

Speaking of rooms, in the context of this book's overarching themes, the concept of a room serves as the liminal space and the interaction between these moments in time that are held in reflection and contemplation. This collection explores themes/motifs of mortality, ephemerality, community, movement/migration, and language, among others, and the concrete connotation that comes with the idea of a physical room is juxtaposed with the more abstract topics within the text, further adding to the intent of liminality, contrast, paradoxes, and transitions.

Furthermore, "room" is also an allusion to Virginia Woolf's extended essay, *A Room of One's Own*, which examines the space—both physical and metaphorical—in which women writers could flourish both intellectually and creatively if given the same opportunities as men in Woolf's time.[1] Though the contemporary writing scene looks vastly different compared to when Woolf wrote, the same ideas about space, belonging, and flourishing continue to stand to this day as we continue to have critical discussions surrounding systemic racism, gender-based violence and oppression, divisions in society, xenophobia, and other pertinent issues regarding opportunity.

Ultimately, *ROOM COLON NINE* is the endlessly paradoxical vertex, or axis, at which beginnings and endings collide, are reconsidered, and are formed anew. The number nine has played a significant role in my life, and I believe that it possesses much meaning regarding the intersections of time, space, belonging, and other philosophical matters that remain painfully relevant in our current day.

---

1 Virginia Woolf, *A Room of One's Own*. New York: Harcourt, Inc., 1929.

TRAJECTORY

Our Beginning

I hope you don't mind the formula I followed.
I brought out the borrowed kayak
from the spider-infested garage; our lifejackets, too.
And I brought us to the mangroves again, where the crabs
swarmed our shadow like the flies back on shore. I brought us
to the beginning, and still there was a hole.
Every voice tells me: to know yourself, you first must know
your roots. I listened to what the King
implored White Rabbit: *Begin at the beginning*.
Translation: begin with a Bang and end quietly—
with a mouth hungering for milk, stumbling through syllables
and our parents' names. I suppose, then, that I am
nearly whole. I suppose I began the right way—
with a story, however crude.
Our mother read folktales to us in our two languages
to say that everyone—every one—has another story.
From the shade of the mangroves, I have pleaded the secrets
of the soil and sea and space but still cannot find my place.
Not every story—journey—has another meaning. Sometimes
I cannot see the stars if I try; sometimes I can when I don't.
The universe is cruel to her inhabitants, but I am not a stranger.
Every story is another story.
Every beginning fears its end; every end fears its oblivion.
I hope I didn't scare you when I leaned over the edge so far
my lips brushed the mossy surface. I promise, it was just
to imagine how far the roots penetrate. Nothing more.
I fear not an end nor an oblivion nor another meaning.
I suppose, now, that I am whole. Hole.

Where We're Headed

I know you might be tired of couplets, but I swear
this isn't another love poem. It's the story

of collarbones unhinging in the absence of their wings
& of dreamers trying to fly using only their ankles & necks.

It's the story of how I bend to the moon
the way she bends to the sea—the way

this house has many windows & still
there is an utter deficiency of light.

In the kitchen, we peel carrots while she tells me
never to apologize for my space. I imagine

how many others once wielded a weapon
just to gather fragments of onomatopoeia

piled up in the sink—porcelain snowstormed
with all those skin cells sloughed off: survival,

an echo of the hurt that comes from falling. I ask
how much longer she thinks I have. *You're already*

a ghost—to hear the promise of homegoing,
& my mouth waters, mother tongue dissolving

further still. We toss the peels & spare green stems,
rinse the edges clean. I pretend that water is just a body,

spinning toward a bigger body. *You, too,*
a collection of particles, wanderer-bound.

Still, I want to believe this migration
carries no more appeal than an afterlife

because we've pointed up at the moon
& her space my whole life as if someday

hoping to fledge. I don't know where we're to go,
don't know if this isolation is only where we belong—

only that all matter in this universe
stumbles & wobbles & dances with chaos,

endlessly confined. & yet, it is here that I learn to love
the taste of dying stars & a changing air,

tongue flowering into the shape of a bird in flight.
& it is in these moments of flocking that I know

we can still be of nature—when the dust lifts
& replaces our bones with breath.

Prologue for the Bird-like Dancer

By morning, the leaves have all
but fluttered down to rest; small migrant
birds fluff their wings and crowd
together in the dirt, emanating petrichor
from a coveted rain. Air crackling
as it dissipates.

And from the skeletal
branches of the cherry tree
in the front yard,
a body has sprung—gray skin split
and drawn across sharp bones,
bare limbs shuddering
in near-silence, almost peacefully.

Following this unconventional method of rebirth
emerges a dancer;

Winter is beautiful enough
to disguise its subcutaneous violence.

And still, dancing
means to have no fear of falling.
It means not looking down
no matter the distance,
measuring and calculating the space around us
from our shadows, our reflections,
and not our figures.
Who are we if not our bodies?

How to emulate the fragility of drying leaves,
        sew moth wings into gossamer gowns—
how to be the wingless bird
and still believe in flying, however futile.

Sometimes belief is all we have left.

The young cherry tree glows dully
in dusk's last light, shadows
and distorted reflections in the frozen puddles
plastered on bark, on body—
body denuded of all those scars, those memories
from winters on winters on winters.

And on the edge of the sidewalk, not far
from the naked cherry tree,
is a bluebird

laying dead on its side by the basketball hoop,
feathers costume-like in arrangement
to preserve what really matters underneath.
What will the other birds do
when they see one of their dead?

And while the night hasn't fully set in,
the migrant birds begin flocking to roost
and those skinny twigs-for-branches
will soon tremble from the weight
of the multitude
of nearly-weightless things—

not a second glance at the ground.
And as the shadows lengthen,

they will dance together
to the gentle sonata that emerges
from the wind and dry branches,
from the fluffing of hundreds of wings
and the hint of petrichor
still in the air.

Chaos Theory

After Salvador Dali's Spider of the Evening *(1940)*

At seven, I was taught the rule of thirds: *Better for the centerpiece*
to be searched for, sky and earth vying for space. Here, the shoreline
of horizon is no place to grow trees, and with the world turning bluer
by the hour, I leave my secrets to the sand: I'm only capable of playing
one song on repeat until I'm vomiting up confessions in D minor. I'm
prone to leaving my neck stranded on high branches when trying to fly
but going again and again—and again and again and again—nonetheless.
I am guilty of loving other girls. I love, loved, have loved. (I live, lived,
have lived.) Now I like to be alone until it suffocates, and only then
am I glad for the body that I have. I believe that sometimes we must cut
off our breasts to get to the heart. And sometimes in the evenings, I wish
for the ants. It is easier now, watching the world without my eyes, nothing
left to weigh. I fold into myself like a book, spine broken—wretched belly
up—since from the way I was tossed, I know I'm meant to scrutinize the fall
through the scope of my navel instead. Oh, the fellow barrenness of the land
is touching. At least I'm not alone. In a nearby corner of the universe, I can
almost hear the angel cursing or uttering a prayer, wings far too small for an
escape. Sometimes being beautiful is all that we have left. I am constantly
thinking about vultures these days, how their tilted wings expertly exert
minimal energy. I watch big black wings descending, almost angelic, and long
to let loose my language, call out for them to take me, though where I search
for lips I find only more yellowed skin and the iron taste of dirt. I, the sun,
dying. We, the people who silenced ourselves too soon. I hear seeing a spider
in the evening is good luck, but I am tired of elegies, of making meaning
out of myth. By now, I've learned to dance with the dead or, at least, for them.
And look, in the distance, there they are, coming closer in the light of dusk's
soft moon, dancing to remind us that this story—mine, yours—is one of hope?

Stars on Sunday

A star came to visit my house last night. It's too bad I don't believe
in wishing. It wasn't smiling or yellow & It didn't twinkle.
It raged in the small space of my bedroom & told me It was dying.
I'm sorry, I awkwardly consoled It, not really knowing what to think.
Cancer, It sighed. I nodded. Are you hungry?
I asked, mostly as a courtesy. It didn't answer,

so we danced instead. Clumsily, like an old couple
not quite remembering the steps but trying desperately
nonetheless. When we both finally fell on the unmade bed,
we giggled in our dizziness like this was a sleepover
& not a goodbye. Control what you can,
It urged, as if reading my mind. Clean off the table
& sweep the floors. Sundays are for cleaning.
Rack dishes & wipe the countertops.
Sundays are for ignoring the apocalypse.

It rained that night—hard enough to console
the burning tree & the burning car down the street.
If the skin can't be mended, it can still be cleaned.
To combat the dimness, I told the star I used to think rain
was god's pee. God's tears sounds more pious,
It replied, & I laughed. I hear the death of a star
is one of the most beautiful moments
in the universe. We pray to dead light
to save our lives. To our ancestors or what we call
a good god:

It's 3am & the dryer rings.
Rang. Is ringing. Inside
is a hole perfect for spinning.
O, look at the mess we're in.

Mess inside us, swallowed up
like an offering or another limb.

There's more than one way to be in love.
We stayed up the rest of the night,
though if we talked much more, I don't remember.
I do remember turning on the shower
& squeezing the bar soap into an
overripe peach. I remember giving It the pit to suck
for keeping the hunger at bay.

Cosmic Wishes: A Metamorphosis

In front of children, I pretend I can understand quantum theory
& even fairytales. *I have three worlds & an imaginary friend.*

    I.
In one, the woman stands beneath the fruit tree.
In this one, no one comes after her, standing so close
their breaths spark & collide.

This is a world that forgets it has dragons.

Rename it *end* so the worst is behind us.

    II.
In another, I watch her watching our neighbors
pack up the moving van from the 2nd floor window.
I touch her shoulder to make sure one of us
is still here.

Her skin, I am told, is an ink printing of dystopia: daughter bowing into earth,
still stinging. A thousand words hewed into gunpowder, or little paper cuts
beneath the breastbone. *This new kind of sadism,* she tells me,
is subversive. Full of sharp shoulders & turned heads.

      Never forget what this world is to you.

      A river, I say dutifully.

This migration is all my body
knows to hold. Most pains leave no scars—

how a tongue will sharpen itself
on the knife that cuts it.

> *& do not forget what you are to it.*

> Stones.

Dreams mold the body into imagination. & anything with a mouth can bite.

Nothing is real, so I cull the bedroom wall
with my teeth, chew plaster. *We're made of empty space,* & I keep going.
The world begins to burn in wildfire.

Beginning
is what we call what we want to forget.

    III.
Stay, she says. I do. She is a good host
& I am a good guest. We dance around each other like strangers
before she beckons me to eat. *Come, let me feed you,*
by which she means, *Let me love you.*

This is what they fed us during the war, she whispers, like it's a secret.
It paints my tongue the way rust would—or my 할머니's old lipliner.
When they die, the meat will be our only monument.

That, & the mouth that bloomed
from the seed that stopped its throat.

Metamorphosis Ghost

I.

On the bank, I practice counting fireflies. Like the stars, they must be too paranoid
to ever be caught still. Dodging scrutiny to maintain that sovereign obscurity
of their timelessness we know so little about.

Above the din of cicadas rides air upon ripples of dark water. Gray breath unfurls:
a suffocating blanket preceding the calm with its urgent prologue.

If quiet enough, pain can reimagine itself for a moment.
If quiet enough, pain can reconfigure skin into ghosts. Forgotten and lingering.

I've counted every breath I've seen
escape my lips—a caravan of ghosts
revealing themselves only upon departure; parasites,
though almost too gentle to be characterized as such,
saying goodbye to a confused host. Still,
they fly away, gauzy and gray and desperate
as though imprisoned by space
itself. Wings still wet and wrinkled from the cocoons.

Aren't you glad to be rid?
I smile / I goodbye / I'm stained red
by the effort.

II.

Somewhere in the distance, an old wind
tiptoes closer to torment—
magnate attracted to movement. So afraid
to touch what it wants; we float
closer to oblivion.

Another breath burgeons

and stops just outside its womb:
another newborn ghost, another lost.

How many more do we have left?
This purging weighs heavily,
and the countdown draws nearer.

One day, the fireflies will be stars, and so will we.
Meaning, we'll become our homes. Skeletal walls
forged from air.

Air, a ghost of one last
attempt to remember
what's been
relinquished.

A metamorphosis
no one recognizes
or remembers,
for we, too,
have become
gauzy.
Gray and desperate
to believe
otherwise.

    III.
whistling wind
stirs the water
once more
disturbing new
wings wanting
to practice
their own
grandiose
escape

and it seems
the whole field
releases a breath
in waiting exposing
gaping dark
lungs of protest
still wrapped
in silk
to the cold—

Mantras of Empty Conviction

On the last day of school, my chemistry teacher told me
that living matter is mostly   empty   space. I stared at him,
eyes   empty, eyes   voids.
So many wings—so many endings—curled into the shudder
of air.   I imagined the atoms   of my body
naked and shivering within, the stupor   burning brightly
behind my eyelids long into June.

      What is real   is relative   is what you make of it.

We come and leave   as ghosts. Groundless and gaunt.
Still, my grandmother wants desperately
to believe in   her god   and not   her ghost.
Let us construct what is real   for ourselves   for once.

      I believe in the forces that tell Daughter to whisper, *It's okay to let   go.*
      So many endings—so many little infinities—between her breaths.

          What is unknown   is all we know.
          What is god   is gone.

Shivering, I touched the skin that was   cold and empty as   space,
and a deathbed just the same, wallowing in the depths.

      In the forces that combat the Oblivion   we carry.
      I, too, am ready to   let   go.   Not entering
      the void, but   leaving it.
      On this path we walk   all alone together.

          What is   the next step   but a
          continuation of our emptiness?
          What is to fear?

Ritual bore the Mother
a nomad   of empty space. I stay tied down   by nothing more
than my faith   in the forces   of nature, of this brief and borrowed existence.

Faith is believing when what is real   screams otherwise;
when what was corporeal   fails to remain.   The body—the spirit—is meant   to be reconfigured.
I   bow deeply, lips twitching   with the all-too-familiar   sting   of salt.
And the world toils toward Chaos, closer still.

Myth of Our Own Meaning

The dead are not dead, just gone, is what we like to say.
You convince yourself of this oxymoron: Odysseus summoned back
Tiresias the prophet & his broken-necked Elpenor; the phoenix was reformed.

The dead are not dead
because we make them so. We pluck new flowers for our altars & graves;
we unfurled celestial utopias out of air & smoke & needing to believe

in *Something* over *Nothing*. We tell the lores of rebirth & wandering ghosts.
Funerals are not for the dead, but for the living.
We aren't scared of death, just of forgetting. Being forgotten.

Just of oblivion.
What is most beautiful—what is most feared—
is what we do not yet know; I write my best poems

in empty rooms or in burned forests, still smoking.
I write in them now, with seared hands, eyes burning. We can be
our own authors & endings.

I taste Frost's warning on the winds of winter: *nothing gold*
can stay. I hear poets romanticizing our hesitancies
into caesuras. Always a diagnosis, always a heroic excuse, for our plight.

There's Elysium & Heaven
& Reincarnation.
There's Tartarus & Hell &

Nothing-Ever-After.
"Utopia" means "Heaven/Elysium
on Earth" means "no place."

& the difference between human & animal is imagination.

Lift your heads out of the haze & grime & watch gravity fall.
I've never heard a plea for this kind of ending, but let me speak it into existence:

Let not the dys-u-topias become more than myth. *No place* must go both ways.
Let not the dead risk changing what's been done. Let not a black hole swallow the earth
without a goodbye. Then let it finally offer us an escape from our terror

disguised as faith. So swallow us whole. Swallow us, hole.
When I am reborn, I will be a bird.
Nothing gold—not quite: nothing at all. Another caesura, another claiming.

Let us find our own meaning, our own ending, beyond the break.
& at least, wings fluttering, let us hope—imagine—that this end is not the End-
All.

Fields and Fields of Dandelions

My friend complains about her short hair when we run, but I secretly
like how freeing it looks. How it looks like a pair of wings someday
hoping to fledge. She has a penchant for electric blue eyeliner
and face tattoos. She tells me she loves boardwalks, and I do, too.
They're the closest we can get to flying, she says.

Though I do believe we can all be equated to birds in some way.
If I am a sora, better at listening, calling, and watching the sky
above, then she is the falcon, the one who climbs to the highest point
only to free fall and catch herself just in time for the ground. The one
who does it again and again and again, dispelling heads of dandelions
with broad black feathers on her way. Sometimes I am lucky enough

to see around the falcon who brings others into her wings to fall and fly.
Sometimes I can see her skin turning into wallpaper, and I admire the way
she once ran fourteen miles in the rain because the music made it beautiful.

Before a race, I once asked her what keeps her going, and she looked at me
and said, *I'm going to Nowhere*. I'm going to know where, someday, we belong.

SPACE, EMPTY

Unmade

The world woke to a spring of feathers tumbling into rain.
I opened my mouth, beckoning the vultures to my throat.

There's part of my body that longed to swallow a beginning
just to see what would happen next. My stomach swelled,

mother's voice carried up from childhood. *There once*
was a girl who plucked out her own feathers

for weaving. / Who else is a girl
trapped in a bird's body? I asked silently.

My own painted back held the answer. Too many times
has mother caught daughter looping talons

through her earlobes. I could not speak if I wanted—throat sewn
shut with twigs. But let me say I am not fit for housing young.

Last April, the chicks all fell from the nest, wet wings tucked
away. I was torpid for days & soon missed the company.

I want to stop wanting—be the one who frees mother bird
from her cage. Mother, who sits alone by the cavern wall.

Let this be a second chance, even if nature doesn't allow
for rebirths. I obsess over endings but am terrified of my own.

I am guilty of knowing that guilt is only where I come from.
I see language for what it is—a circumvention—& bleed out

for the price of my thoughts in couplets & preemptive elegies.
In imagining infinity, lonely, waiting to be touched. I want a world

with no more hands, wings stitched together again with red thread
& a needle thin enough to gather nectar. I promise to tuck what's left

back in the sewing kit & leave us alone with our holes
& our holiness. & this is how I know a body without its mouth

is always searching for a river. Not to heal,
but to taste an earth like the one it once knew.

I Hear They Make Marionettes That Fly Now

Time travel is real, the body imaginary, & anything short-lived
is worth its inception. Last words lay down our claim to the land

we're buried in. The more I travel, the more I crave home,
& so my brother & I are like crows on the bus—beaks clacking, wings flapping,

talking about everything & saying nothing at all. Where is your language?
An old 할아버지 asks me. It's in my back pocket, I want to say with my stolen words.

I keep it there for extra cushion & because it's too beautiful to keep in my mouth,
but I don't tell him that. I laugh instead, & between my teeth are glossy black feathers

plucked from my own back. I know we do not belong here. I know my coppered hands
gave us away. Anything with a mouth is dangerous, & language is everything

we know we cannot keep. It's the most beautiful part of my body
because it was the first to escape & the first to be buried.

I wore a mask for months after the pandemic was over.
I should've realized the silence of the spaces we inhabit—how the stars

aren't meant to be wished upon or prayed to, despite their radiance.
How they're the dregs, the backwash, of the universe.

What does that make us? I once asked.
Frauds.

Now I'm in the backyard where we buried—maybe too aggressively—
the chestnuts & watermelon seeds that never grew.

Where we arranged the broken shells to make a beach
surrounded by dandelions. I blow, & I am thinking about the bird

who collided with our kitchen window this morning.
Perhaps when I ran to her, she wasn't dead, just stunned. All I had to do

was breathe beneath her feathers to resuscitate,
but all my mouth knew to do was suck in & swallow.

How to distance myself enough from what I am: a raven
or a tricky horizon riddled with instinct. How a redder sun this morning

wasn't from a new turn of the earth
so much as the sky & sea declaring exile.

For the Siren, Alone, on the Hill

I confess that, at sixteen, I am still afraid of holding my breath
in front of the mirror. That, & hide-&-seek

after dusk. Anything can transform
under the right moon, which is to say, anything is a wolf

to us birds. When the pipes cracked in October & pummeled
the drywall, B & I skated around the barren hardwood

in frayed socks. We fell & didn't get back up—there was no reason
to stand. Like all exiles, we slithered until someone shrieked

& got the broom, then hid in the closet until the house
emptied. Until we could grow peacock feathers

pretty enough to fool whoever else
was predator. During this time, we built card houses

& sipped green tea—mostly for show—
& licked another corner free of cobwebs

whenever hunger threatened to give us away;
men in dark robes came & went, scampering like rats

behind a velvet curtain. We were deathly
still. They turned up pointed noses, no doubt

sniffing the stale air for a confession. Perhaps
a baby's palm or gauzy cocoon, abandoned

in the flood. The mover's truck came eventually,
but still we did not bother to unfurl ourselves—

even when they choked on dead names. Just stayed holed up

in that holey place for a while longer. Like a church.

Garden

By the end of winter, the plants that have survived in our house are the cacti and plastic roses
in the kitchen. We have about ten tulips in our front yard and proudly call it a garden.
All autumn, my dad lovingly sculpted the gentle earth into an armory, front-line shields
of pine straw on dusty white bulbs. Still, the raiders / the survivors fool our hands, an earthy trap.
Survival worships the hungry, chasing striped tails into the wintery bushes near the sidewalk.
Meanwhile, a resplendent display of soldiers rots in the ground. Bite marks plague instead of bullets,
but I suppose I can't begin to equate the two. Somewhere, the ground is wet and fertilized with blood.
Feign ignorance and wait for spring. Rivulets of melted snow carve the hard dirt into valleys,
into trenches. Peace is in burned trunks and stained grass. In the still-smoky air above
the *what-was* garden. In the dirt, whose ravaged body becomes a mosaic of boot prints.
Peace in pieces at our feet. Memory of marches, biting into bulb / bursting breast. If not graveyard,
say *memorial of just-barely survivors.* After the gelid air subsides, the womb of the earth erupts.
And our tulips shake their heads free of dirt, already bowing to the next rain.

Notes on Surviving

In our empty house, my 할머니 fills the glass cabinet with drinking cups,
adorned with white-and-gold birds that seem to always hold their necks

above the waterline. To bring in the New Year, we drink from these cups
to pretend that we, too, can float on weightless wings. To pretend that these birds

aren't drowning to satisfy our needs. Masters of poker, of concealment.
Masters of none. Thin, hollow-boned magpies whose skin gasps

when the wind blows, as if our lungs alone can't satisfy
just how much breath we need to keep moving.

We have been stripped of our feathers, you see, mouths sharpened
to aquiline points. No one talks about the scars that beauty

leaves behind, or the guise. Without our wings, we suddenly want so badly
to fly, fleshy wing-buds reminiscing the ghost of wind on long flight feathers.

Two phantom limbs taking up space. Let's submit instead to a mouth
that's ready to prick and preen and perfect a meaningless life, the only useful part

of our body left. Still, we are my 할머니's birds. We are not known here for our beauty,
but for our persistence, straining delicate vertebrae above the rising water

despite the distance. Was she so wrong for wanting to escape?
I know I've inherited this migratory instinct.

We've made machines that speak our success into existence,
mouths assuming the job of our wings.

Speaking must mean we make bridges with our tongues
and break them with our teeth, with what's left.

We have learned to make do without our hands like birds,
only it's said that birds are free because they fly.

I say they fly because they cannot bear
to feel the roughness of the ground their whole lives.

Ode to River Currents

I don't believe a day goes by that escapes the river.
You do not have to be good to be taken by its water.
I know many saved & many drowned, & I shiver,
Though the air steams. What can heal can also slaughter.

There is no one around to watch as I approach
The banks. There is no one to witness or endanger
The beckoning hand that emerges, no one to reproach
Me for trusting a stranger. It was not a stranger.

Hand beckons. I follow. Hand grips hand, sweating
Off the grime. Hand pulls & calls another wave
Around us, my body a child's stick in the sand. Letting
Myself go is not an escape, I know. & *brave*
Is the one who resists the comforts of the deep
Where creatures simply wake & live & sleep.

Above me, the surface is still, obsidian in the night,
Reflecting the glare of the houses crowded on the shores.
Low branches in the wind wobble & whine; despite
A burning of the lungs, I could stay here, watch the oars
Churn the surface above & the hooks steal buckets of blood.
I could wake & live & sleep & escape the flood.

But if the path to peace is a natural one,
Then let it be found in the absence of light.
Let it be found far from shore, out where none
But the herons fly—long after the houses, burning and bright.
And it's here I'd know we can still be of nature: when the sky grieves
And my skin disappears into shadows, into ripples, into leaves.

Body, the Antithesis of Language

I am afraid of heights, my bedroom after 4pm, heartbeats,
dark streets with bright lights, intestines, goodbyes,
and the ever-turning, self-fulfilling entropy of the universe.

I begin this poem with a confession because the funny
thing about confessions is that they're the impostors
of language. What I mean is, we confessionalists

love to lament our endings, but all language is a little birth
and a little death, every word in-between bloodlessly
revealed. I am only sure of two other things: that life

is just one enduring argument with the weather
and that nourishment is to the stomach its long slow
death. Too often do I look to the plants for inspiration,

wishing I never had to hear the sounds of my teeth
as they gnash the remains of the living. Or the gulping,
choking sounds of living particles being sucked

down the esophagus and into the pit. I might be deathly
afraid of heights. Afraid of falling. Afraid of my feet
on the ground but the inner platform crumbling.

I once heard that when water doesn't have enough oxygen,
fish will swim to the surface and gulp down bubbles
of air. I am thinking of all the times I mistook the dying

for a spectacle. I am thinking of all the times
watery secrets floated like bubbles above my head,
the living so close I could almost smell them.

I am thinking of the liminal space in which life is lived

the way it would if the world were just beginning,
if the world were ending, if the world were already

gone. It's here I discover that pain is the language
of the body and silence is the language of the mouth,
enemy of the mind: I confess I am afraid of confessions

because they are always filled with ghosts.
The kind of ghost that mourns near rivers
and candle lit windows at dusk. The kind of ghost

that can only lament the mere echo of breath.
I confess that all the streets I know are filled
with ghosts. On these streets, I watch people

walking in their own cloud of air, the only proof
that they are living. Breath: one last sacrifice
so that we could live.

Imagining infinities

"Some infinities are bigger than other infinities" - John Green, *The Fault in Our Stars*

        we have found solace
in this one moment, whose standstill is wholly an interim/infinity,
imagine:
        our breath/,
        the river that spills and tumbles/,
        the dying star frozen mid-supernova...
that we have found our infinity in knowing
that everything leaves
before it dies:

        in the space between the wood and the lights
of a dancing stage, there is a mountain whose boulders
balance perfectly on the precipice.
most peculiar how, amidst the indistinguishable chatter
of a waiting audience,
there is evidence of an ocean's grainy water
still tossing and turning about the sandy shore at night
in the breath of a performer/performance
chafing the eardrum.

remember this:
she (and by *she*, i mean the dancer/everybody/you)
once thought we were all just ourselves,
but perhaps *identity* is made up of who we inhabit—
a collection of millions of tiny lives
all living under one name.
        because, we whisper,
        all the way across every pore
        on our skin, *we just want to survive.*

after all, she is more than rivers and forests and beaches,

just as skin is a mosaic
made strong by protests.
like the leaves and the grains of sand,
the dying seagrass and mountain pebbles,
this skin/painting/costume
becomes new every seven years—
this body will be ours/a stranger (again).

and so: this girl walks on dancing feet
beside the river close to her home,
fingertips/fingerprints brush cold currents/entrails.
both hold their breath/life
upon touching emptiness.
she and *they* are nearly synonymous,
living a shared life
neither can claim to/or understand:

but too late: another breath/life
has seen what it is made of.
you have frightened your body
into believing
it is real/what is real/nothing is real:

maybe we are all attracted to things
that will destroy us in the end.
we are made of what's left of stars
after they die;
we are born from a destruction called
the most beautiful phenomenon in space
and have lived its mirror image faithfully
on earth.
maybe beauty outruns all,
even in death—especially in death—
in our experimental understanding
of ourselves.

and so: she looks back upon
what she has made/been part of,
scanning her skin for signs of creation.
she watches as pores open up,
expand to form stars/holes/nothings again,
      the mosaic finally breaking.

and a crescendo rises from the rivers and tall grasses,
from the forests and washed-over-but-still-partly-existing
shores, the mountain whose boulders
begin to fall, its cave
a mouth—opened and ravenous.
then the tail-end ringing reverberates,
and she can still hear/feel its echo
      in the rattle of breath,
      in the slight shake of hand,
      in the vibration of vocal folds,
after everything is still/dead/itself (again).

What was in Reverse

Tonight, I mistake the fire hydrant for a gravestone
& taste your voice peeling itself off the back of my throat.

Read *esophagus*—jargon I concoct into meaning.
Gravestones should never be bare,

so I fist dandelions between swollen knuckles
to offer my condolences & release around my shadow

in some twisted wreath. A ghost is only a ghost
when there's someone left to remember.

& I bend because bowing is the only way
to console the earth for our collective weight.

& because good gifts come in pairs,
I blow out a breath & leave the crescendo behind

to rattle in a mason jar, reminded of the fireflies
I caught & kept just a moment too long.

& just like that, my throat balloons into gizzard, only good
for jokes & turning heads. I begin collecting rocks

in my stomach to keep from wasting away & laughing
with the sting of descent. I remind myself

to tuck glass jars beneath my eyelids,
just to see how much I can take. I want

to forget how to swim & how to sink—see the world
in all its liminal space. I believe the moon offers more excuses

than the sun for my rootless ways: On sleepless nights,
I was told there was a rabbit in the moon, but to me

there was only ever fish & hook.
People tell me, *You're good with smiles /*

similes. Mask melded into skin.
Shaped like a stranger I stopped to talk to

& got to know a little. Or a chain
around a tongue once suckled, once claimed.

WHAT SHALL WE DO WITH THE CATTLE?

Aubade for Our Stars

We the People of the United States, in Order to form a more perfect Union, establish Justice, [...] and secure the Blessings of Liberty to ourselves and our Posterity, do ordain and establish this Constitution for the United States of America.

Last night, I killed another spider. Stole her web
with dirty hands and watched as soap and hot water
cleaned them again. The age-old remedy of gods
is erasure. & slow death still means more life—
right?

      We the People of the United States
must have faith in what we've stolen.

Cue the blood & bruises—in red & white & blue—
from people crushing people to catch the verdict:
Guilty.

To whom can we turn now
for what is good? The path to righteousness is shifting,
& we metamorphosize into hunting dogs, keen to follow the scent.
      in Order to form a more perfect Union,
Taste on the wind the frozen embryos
—the citizens—near the place where
men are crucified, gurney-like. Mothers behind doors,
children wear the mask.
A n y l a s t w o r d s ?
      establish Justice,
P r a y f o r m e .
      & secure the Blessings of Liberty
This earth is not ours.
      to ourselves & our Posterity,

Still, we tossed the crucifixion to the dogs & smoke, all that was left.
The soil beneath soft as a sponge & sticky with spit.
There are no resurrections for the damned, only for the damn-
ers. Decay is still time spent with the earth.
& we swaddled the embryos
in the law & loving arms.

We the silence-of-allies. *We* the world-afraid
-of-a-god's-poker-face.

How everyone—every one—turned & fled
at the first whiff of real flesh. & the way we blamed
the screams & pressing hands on the wind
& a trick of light—

   do ordain & establish this Constitution
   for the United
   States of America.

Dystopian Agenda for an American Night

This evening, there will be one last soundtrack on the cycle of stars.
Instead of songs, only a muted whisper of the torment
will be left. An elegy for the end of the world.

Where hounds on ramshackle porches will howl up at the sky
in painful reverence, tasting the sharpness of the symphony
cut their tongues.

At midnight, a reckless chariot will tumble out of the moon
onto the mortal ground it had refused to aid. It will lust still
for the nectar of the sky.

Yes, hunger will corrode stomach before skin
so that we may still appear satiated. So that we may not complain again
about ever being empty.

The tired poet will keep churning out lyrics on the stage:
"can we not have the solace / of sleep?" & we will will cheer
for their suffering, mistaking it for passion.

There will be no memorials
for the survivors of this night, only for the dead.
There will be no memorials left.

We will wake to the sun & moon waving goodbye.
To the now-quiet dogs wet with dew.
To the water reflecting what stars are left.

Hubcaps & other miscellaneous metal bits
catch the light in the foil of greenery,
wreckage of the tragic chariot.

We will wake with our faces indented

by couch cushions, the remote at our fingertips,
Another accident on I-85. Two dead. But don't worry—

we can shut it off at any time.
We will wake to the banner of stars above the yard, saluting.
And from the ground, we proclaim emptiness to be the home of gods.

What Lives

Her baby's born at midnight, open-mouthed to the sea.
　　　The suspended moon longs for slumber. / Below, a hushed world
　　　understands the gravity, so the tide enters quickly,
　　　stealing the bodies it dropped as it leaves.
　　　Death? Or rebirth? / Wonder who chose the tragedy.
New diaphragm experiments amidst the eerie mist
of the bay nearby. She soon utters out a still portrait, unfinished portrait,
into the night, the jargon slippery on a moistened tongue:

　　　Of *slippery bodies clustered together*
　　　at an overcrowded puddle, roiling waves of hunger
　　　pummeling each esophagus. Stomachs heaving,
　　　stilling, surrendering to their veneration
　　　despite the discomfort. Wet skin shrivels,
　　　reaching up

　　　to where lives are better in our imaginations.
Last night, four kids hurtled down
the narrow Kirkland street,
a flaming vessel of destruction.
By mid-afternoon, red and yellow flowers
in plasticky wrap embellish the ravaged, feral trunk.

Death is when there's no one left to remember /
when everyone else remembers to remember.

　　　Of *in the darkness, dull moonlight*
　　　uncovers the robbed belly;
　　　the sandy, half-buried limbs;
　　　mouth opened in prayer to the shifting tide.

In what could be warzone, soft cradle arms
offer up their empty carriage to next rainfall. /

Lamentations are for the living.
     Carry us to the sea.

At midnight, a child died on Kirkland street
while [I] brushed [my] teeth
and worried about how many tests [I] had in school.

How [I] twisted the faucet and turned the water
while the burning vessel thundered and cried
and offered up a heavy downpour of powdered glass.

[I] imagine the pieces
reflected the glow of the streetlights.
And the red and white and blue. Hear: anthem of hunger.

Bleeding stomach ousted unfinished womb
into the street—paint-splattered, tortured, seaside artist
screaming in the night.
Somebody's baby.

     Of *under the stars, she enters*
     touching sand, clingy with dampness.
     Viscous and heaving,
     the reddening vessel
     keens, slowly settling into silence.
     Still, she's done her job.

Everything that lives dies / that dies lives. /
Living is birthed from the womb of the dying and the dead.

     Of *Deliverer.*
     Unwanted/unwonted vessel of creation.
     Leaking ashes onto the birthbed.

Confessions from the Angels of Ephemerality

Already, I am reaching
out to you, arms quivering as air. Admitting Last Words
is never easy.
     Imagine your bodies into something beautiful,
our dance teacher squawked.
Lacing fingers into wind, the little birds and butterflies
sucked in their stomachs.
     We want our dancers to look the same, make no mistake.
An army of angels lost amidst the snow-
covered skyline.

Starving in their gossamer costumes, the winged creatures hovered above us
just out of reach. A safe distance, but close enough to admire
nonetheless. Enthralled, I suppose—but never sadistic.

I have, here, a world
that does not even know the difference.
Only difference.

In the audience, we silently lamented our dull bodies.
And yet, our distance from nature is our invention.
Let us unveil the vexing history
of *we*, the motherland deserters.

From the ground, the migration toward earth proved
a breathtaking spectacle: We craned our necks
to the thousands of birds and butterflies
free falling toward earth
like meteors or bombs.

I have a world
that does not mind the difference.

War gets the last word, and so,
tarnished and bleeding, the dance ended
all too soon. Yet joyously, we wept, brandishing
plastic bags to collect the jewels of our destruction—
pardon me, *invention*—all strewn
about the wasteland.

Our distance from nature is our greed.
The earth hinges on its axis toward longevity, but this we can combat:

> *I, too, sat through the whole show—masquerade—in stockings*
> *and a new dress. And when I clapped, my hands*
> *thundered like war.*

Snapshots

February Atlanta sunlight cuts sharply through the window disguising the cold
A room shrouded behind thicketed pine needles   from the road   a rogue star
spinning wildly to its own orbit, to the beat of five o'clock traffic

Somewhere, a chubby fist chokes a red crayon   and draws the sun
Somewhere, a camera crew follows a matriarch leading the herd to a generational waterhole
They come away disappointed   On returning, they pass dry sun-bleached sticks & bow
to the bones & the audience waits with bated breath
Nature decrees &   we obey & — right?

Somewhere, a man paces the corner in front of a church   blistered feet in canvas shoes
burning with cold   Under self-constructed constellations,
he, too, recites the lines of an ancient play   but for no audience
except the two a.m.   stragglers on the road   providing a lonesome chorus
Why have a voice   if no one believes you?

Somewhere, hands yank children out of strollers   rushing to the safety of their—
the fire/   the gunman/   the end of the world behind them tucked safely into a letter
of goodbye
I mean, elegies for the guilty

Through the bedroom window   quilted sky sews itself back together
around the thin branches of pine trees, illuminating wind-bent trunks   & woodpecker holes

Somewhere, a news anchor gels hair & paints mouth   & smiles blindingly into the camera
before reporting the updates   of the most recent—
& pictures of razed cities from the TV blow languidly   into the air supply
following the weather report;   we gasp then resume/we are wont
Somewhere, dry hands hang the laundry   at midnight

But here, shafts of evening sunlight   play hide-&-seek
with the spiderwebs who've glued themselves   to every ceiling corner
& bookshelf of the bedroom

That's all it is/we are/we see: a snapshot   of disbelief

Somewhere, a giant hand reaches for a fine-point pen & adds the finishing touches
to the newest cosmic comic, vol. 23, "special edition"—& we sigh with the recapitulation
Somewhere, our orbit continues, an intricate waltz uninterrupted by the hand.

Somewhere   here   there   is   only   emptiness

Plight of the captive fish

here are the fish tanks by the window,
with their cheap plastic coral bits and shipwrecks
so delicately positioned,
allow me to show you around:
ocellaris clownfish, bettas, goldfish—

all fragile and armor-bodied,
all beautiful and part of the masses

      there is wonder enmeshed in the unreadable

but let me make this clear:
we are not above this scaled plight,
our only difference being
that we're just larger fish in a larger bowl,
thinking that it's the ocean,
that we're free

i watch the clownfish make a kissing face against the glass
and i think it, too, must have made a wish

just as i turn the same seashell around in my hands
from many years past
again and again
      this is the same as saving great swathes of photographs
      from childhood—not for beauty but for comfort in preservation
feeling its exacting grooves
retrace their memories onto my brain
along with the wishes

am i now so forgetful that the most mundane object
still captivates?

or perhaps i just can't fathom
how an object so well-traveled
has no mystery left for us—this story could mirror
that which belongs to the sea:

> *a mother making her way up the beach at night*
> *to nest, wet skin & shell plastered with shavings*
> *from that moonlit studio floor*
> *she dodges the silvery bodies of floundering minnows*
> *left behind by the waves*
> *with the tidiness & accuracy*
> *of a practiced figure of the shore*
>
> *no more a sculptor than a sculpture,*
> *no more creator than creation*

i wonder which kind of life
the fish back in the city tanks would prefer:
to wish, in a twisted way, for a predictable ending /

or to risk being like those creatures of silvery treasure
drying slowly on the shore, retaining a surging memory
of vast, grainy expanses
of overpowering waves

of taking the shell once more in their/your/my hands,
now knowing that an object so well-traveled
must have some mystery left

> *& out where the gulls cry louder than the wind,*
> *the aged sculptor of the waves*
> *continues to carve away great,*
> *crumbling pieces from her crude sculpture*
> *& even the distant trees*
> *bow deep & slow in reverence,*
> *foreseeing a preeminent retelling*
> *of creation*

Essence of an Ant(i) Life

The papers tell of people dropping dead as fast as the fire spreads.
On the news, a boy is slowly starving. He shows his
empty stomach and rotting ribs to the world, as if telling us to stare,
and we do, mesmerized.
A movement, you say pityingly from the comfort of the couch.
But there's a fine line between genius and madness.
Stop quoting clichés.
Hunger reminds us that we are alive;
quietly, then all at once.

and in this way,
pain is the next closest thing to language:
articulate and glaring
and yet, no one knows what it really has to say,
so they'll nod and say *i'm sorry,*
but to be so honest with you
none of this is real
they will say *remember that everything*
on this planet
is empty space
little particles in a vast_____ of emptiness:
they will utter a satire, an elegy
for mother earth, the prophet
for humanity, the ignorant oracle

and so we will protest: *you're wrong!*
so keen to deny what we already know
emptiness is too simple a word;
there is no word for this world

and in this way,
i mean that pain is the opposite of language
i mean that it embraces what cannot be conveyed

i papier-mâché my bruised bones, cracked bones
into a mosaic of self-pity
and watch from afar as the fire bestows itself
upon the ravaged land

oh, what to call this
but a war of worlds / of words /
of the time we humans feared our language
and so we lusted for the smoke and fire
to sooth our empty stomachs instead

The (Dream)world in Which a Fear of Insects is Not Enough

& all at once, the bedroom has become a garden of skittering bodies.
In the darkness, you can feel the legs scrabbling at your dry skin & bamboo hair.
Why must they contort in the face of Death? They're crawling into your mouth,
& you have no choice but to swallow: *Be silent. It's—too—*
late. But already, you hunger for what the human spirit has become:
an instrument of destruction.
   Starvation is unforgiving & so are we.
    We close our eyes & forget.

You sing & spiral & scream & forget to breathe;
Death continues to count out Its days;
& all the while, the antennae spin wildly in protest
against the ridges of your throat & into your stomach
as you gasp, flailing for the inner reaches of imagination, of ignorance,
   dreaming of Dreamlessness once again,
    like a fractured, bleeding, ill-fated
     roach in a trap.

But who are the dying ones? You ask. *Thousands,* I admit. *Millions*
who won't care for your dreams when your mind is the worst that has hurt you.
Keep repeating this monologue of denial. / "Just close your eyes."

Already, it is—too—late.
Death reminds us what matters

after the fact.
& still, the hope that this greedy Mouth will spare Its devouring instinct
for you, alone, for once—you who turned your face from the sight of blood—
will drop & shatter the way one falls out of a Dream:

     Unforgiving, & all at once.

Food Poison

In the rusty dregs of the 순두부찌개, I glimpse my grandmother
in my own hands. She bends over the stone bowl to scrape up
the last of the rice. A sculptor of suffering
scavenging food into a prayer. She eats the answers
before she hears them.

> By morning, another truck sends for the cows. The old mothers
> whose utters sag, whose skins drag from the weight
> of the faint whisper of babies.
> *Tell me, mother: why is it we were born into our bodies?*

From the table, I see practiced bodies tossing pans,
laughing and swaying aproned hips to the K-pop
on the radio and sizzling skin.

> Ours are special. special special SPECIAL
> our special sacrifice.
> *Mother, this is snake-talk.*

The steam from the burning soup breathes harshly in my face.
I cannot open my mouth. My own skin falls in, boiling with the rest.
And so we're slowly killing ourselves,
eating because we're desperate not to die.

> Feet scrabble on the metal floor of the truck,
> skinny body against body, bone bruising bone.
> *Mother, I am hungry.*

but / *but*

i can't eat in this slaughterhouse of civility
    i didn't want to see this

it was just to stay alive—

    is everything for hunger?—

what choice did i have betrayed by my own snake tongue?—

    —and what is a body but someone else's blessing?

GOING, GOING

Origins

"The most beautiful part of your body / is where it's headed" - Ocean Vuong

We came into this world wanting—
what is beautiful. I mean when we wailed cryptic confessions
into our mother's ears in the sleepless early hours and the times
we caught the ocean, jaws unhinged against the skyline,
swallowing the sun just minutes too late; when what I mean of *we*,
unbound by borders; when the waves turn a violent, beautiful gray
in the first summer storm & when the trees
bow to their roots in the wind; when, in the last shards
of sunlight, we bare our teeth into the curve of the earth
& turn to animals in the still heat of twilight.
Nothing can touch us, we scream
into the waves, & in this brief haze,
we are right. We come & leave from water,
not from dust. Sea-womb, see womb,
mother of mothers. Our histories rise & foam & crash
again & again. Cogency is not an enemy
of instinct, just its rival. Every moment has since
suspended itself before free fall.
Let us rise & wait & crash.
Let us break
& reform.
This, too, can be a new
beginning. I can wade in the oblivion
that's become so hungered for. It brings me
before the ground—reminds me that respite
is only temporary. Bowing low, I rake the earth
with cracked teeth, my body lulled once more
into instinct—into memory—by the silence of the sea / see.
Let us move beyond our fixture on endings, it seemed to whisper
—& we left the same way.

Somehow, Someday

I won't turn away from the nightmare
where I am the only one left in my home.
Where I wander, where I dig & dig & dig,
where my tears tear gashes in the red clay,
clearing it of all remaining mystery. It knows
I hunger for a restart. Someday, I think I'll love
how love appears, all disguised. *Those who wander
are not lost.* Those who wander are conjuring up ways
to go, to let go, when what's inside is no more.
Let's chase what we're missing like the falling leaves
we used to catch for luck. Now this poem has more
endings than autumn, words tumbling & halting
into a waterfall's icy gathering of uncertainty.
When you approach its edge, wondering what's below
—what's beyond—remember wishing for your future
is almost nostalgia. Remember how the sun sighed
a mosaic of a story each night before falling
or how your mother looked when you first left home.
Let's remember how the cold buried itself into your skin
after jumping through the mountain spray. Sometimes pain
does us good—reminds us we're still alive: Someday,
I'll come to love my paper-cut scars & too-short nails,
bad haircuts & moving days. Not every dream
has a consequence. Many can somehow return
to the womb, dormant. But I try to imagine the ones
that do fly. Exit wounds are homages to every-
thing that's already departed. All cells come
from other cells, I tell the wandering.
What's inside is always more—& good
at returning. Someday, I'll love what newness
blooms beneath. Someday, I'm told I'll love
how everything leaves & always ends.

If Ceiling Fans Could Talk

I hang from the cracked white ceiling, watching every morning unfold like a letter. I rarely see anyone's face—only the clock's and those hoping to find answers written somewhere above them. I have watched countless bodies come and go. My job is simple: turn the air, mimic the wind. I know that people long for what they do not have. In summer, they complain the room stifles them, but in the winter, they pull my string, let me lie still and let the dust gather. This room was not always the same. It used to be a house, an old, traditional one. Before the walls were knocked down, carpets laid. Red brick painted white, new schoolhouse. Still, I hang up on the ceiling and remained unchanged. I'm tired of being a wallflower, of making ghoulish shadows on this plain ceiling, of spinning noisily and being utterly forgotten. A typical day goes like this: I'm usually woken up at around 8:00 AM in warm months but in the afternoon in winter. I listen to the sound of the computer until the stampede at 8:30 AM of students trying not to be late. Then someone always complains about the temperature. Then sometimes I'm turned off because the heater is broken in the building (this is not uncommon). Steps three and four are repeated several times a day. On and off. Off and on. Five days a week, thirty-six weeks a year. But I suppose, in some ways, I'm lucky. I love the way this room smells like old books. I am fortunate to know the words of Wordsworth, Whitman, and Dickenson; I know Kafka and Shakespeare and Achebe; I know the secrets of writing good dialogue and what makes poetry beautiful and the utterly irresistible pull of a good novel. I know the passion of a good teacher and her students. Sometimes, after the doors lock for the summer, I think that there are worse fates than being a ceiling fan.